Weighty Words, Too

WEIGHTY WORDS, TOO

Paul M. Levitt
Elissa S. Guralnick
Douglas A. Burger

Illustrations by
Katherine Karcz

University of New Mexico Press

Albuquerque

Text © 2009 by Paul M. Levitt, Elissa S. Guralnick,
and Douglas A. Burger
Illustrations © 2009 by Katherine Karcz
Printed in Malaysia by TWP America, Inc.

21 20 19 18 17 16   2 3 4 5 6 7

LIBRARY OF CONGRESS CATALOGING-IN-PUBLICATION DATA
Levitt, Paul M.
Weighty words, too / Paul M. Levitt, Elissa S. Guralnick,
Douglas A. Burger ; illustrations by Katherine Karcz.
        p. cm.
Summary: Provides definitions for twenty-six vocabulary
words from "aggrandizement" to "zany" with stories
containing puns that provide mnemonic devices for
remembering the definitions.
ISBN 978-0-8263-4558-5 (printed case : alk. paper)
1. Children's stories, American. [1. Short stories.
2. Vocabulary. 3. Puns and punning. 4. Mnemonics.]
I. Guralnick, Elissa S. II. Burger, Douglas A.
III. Karcz, Katherine, ill. IV. Title.
PZ7.L5824Wg 2009
[Fic]—dc22

                    2008031012

Designed and typeset by Mina Yamashita: Text composed
in Kepler Std., a contemporary typeface designed by Robert
Slimbach for Adobe, with display type in Jimbo designed
by Jim Parkinson.

Contents

A Aggrandizement 3

B Burdensome 7

C Criterion 11

D Destination 14

E Exonerate 19

F Furbelow 23

G Geniality 26

H Hibernate 29

I Improbable 32

J Jeremiad 35

K Katzenjammer 39

L Lackadaisical 42

M Mystify 46

N Nadir 51

O Optimum 53

P Partisan 57

Q Querist 60

R Rusticate 63

S Surreptitious 67

T Tirade 69

U Utilize 72

V Vicarious 77

W Wondrous 79

X Xerophyte 82

Y Yokefellow 85

Z Zany 89

A

When Ezra and Ethel Ermine won a fortune in the lottery, they decided to change their way of life.

"It's time we left our hole in the ground," said Ethel. "I'm ready to move to the city and live in a house."

"I agree," said Ezra, "but let's buy one large enough to impress the whole neighborhood." And so, without even saying good-bye to their old friends, they moved. Not into a bungalow. Not into a townhouse. Not into a condominium with a swimming pool and tennis courts. No, they moved into a mansion.

"Jeepers, creepers!" said Ethel. "How will I ever keep up with the cleaning?"

"With parlor maids and kitchen girls," said Ezra proudly.

Why, they even hired a cook, then invited Lady Moneybags for lunch. They wanted her

4

to help them plan a dance for their wealthiest neighbors. Only the richest people would be invited. But Lady Moneybags warned them that everything would have to be perfect: the food, the music, and, most of all, the house, which needed decorating. Ethel set to work at once. She sewed old bedspreads together and hemmed them for drapes. She also wove rush mats for the floors. Meanwhile, Ezra built a dining table from wooden crates and made mirrors by polishing pieces of tin. In the middle of the living room, the Ermines installed a stove, since April could be chilly and they didn't want their guests to be cold. They made pillows out of burlap for their guests to sit on. Last but not least, they purchased a player piano with lots of rolls of ragtime tunes so everyone could dance the night away.

But in spite of all these careful preparations, on the night of the ball, no one danced. No one ate. No one sat on the pillows made of burlap, or glanced into the mirrors made of tin. The guests had no sooner arrived than they turned on their heels and walked out with a humph—all except Lady Moneybags, who stayed just long enough to explain why the ball was a flop.

"You see," she explained, "when people of importance mention a drape, what they mean is not a bedspread cut to cover up a window, but a lovely piece of velvet hanging gracefully from ceiling to floor. And when they speak about a mirror, what they mean is not polished tin dangling from a string, but a silvered glass set in a frame. And when they speak about a covering for the floor, what they mean is not a mat that has been woven out of rush, but a Persian carpet made from soft, thick wool."

"I think I understand," said Ezra, as he slumped on the piano bench. "When people of importance speak of a piano, I guess they aren't thinking of an old battered upright that plays by itself."

"No, indeed," said Lady Moneybags coldly.

"When the rich and the powerful speak of a piano, you can be sure that a grand is meant."

So, whenever someone gains (or seeks) power and wealth, think of Lady Moneybags saying, "a grand is meant," and you will remember the word

AGGRANDIZEMENT

B

John Harmony's pet parrot Polly had been raised in a small English village. But unlike any of the parrots in London—or for that matter, anywhere else in the world—Polly could add, subtract, multiply, and divide long numbers in her head, even when the numbers had decimal points. She could manage fractions, too, as well as calculus. What's more, she wrote poetry with lines like

> I think that I shall never see
> A sticky wicket lovely as a tree.
> > or
> Wee Willie Winkie made himself a pest
> Running through the village in his red vest.

Polly, in fact, had only one defect: she had trouble pronouncing her *r*'s and her *w*'s.

When Polly added two and one, she said the answer was "thwee." And when she multiplied two times ten, the answer she came up with was "trenty." As for her poetry, she could hardly recite it well when she ended up saying, "A sticky ricket lovely as a twee" or "Ree Rillie Rinkie." But for years there was nothing to be done about the problem. Polly, you see, was enormous and couldn't sit on John Harmony's shoulder while he rode his red horse to Banbury Cross, where the speech teacher gave lessons. She would have had to have been carried in a cart, but John Harmony couldn't afford one.

Imagine his joy, then, when an old uncle gave him a cart as a present. Finally, Polly

could be driven to the speech lessons that John so badly wanted her to have.

But on the Monday morning when John set out toward Banbury Cross for the first of Polly's lessons, a farmer from a nearby village stood in the road and held up his hand.

"John, John! I need your help. My wagon's been stolen, and I have to find a way to send my cabbages to market. Will you take them in your cart to Banbury Cross?"

John agreed to take as many crates as he could carry. Ten fit nicely. But when Polly sat down on the cabbages, the cart collapsed under the weight of the load.

Poor John nearly cried. But the farmer said, "Never you mind, young man. I'll get my tools and fix what's broken." In only a few hours, the cart was repaired.

"Luckily," said John, "we left early. We'll still be arriving at Banbury Cross in time for Polly's speech lesson."

"I'm delighted," said the farmer, "but couldn't you please take at least a few crates of cabbages in the cart? I would surely be grateful if you'd try to carry some."

John put five crates in the cart. But once Polly climbed in, the little red horse couldn't pull the heavy load.

The farmer asked him to haul just three crates or two. But even one proved too heavy for the little red horse once Polly jumped on board.

"I wish I could help," John said sadly to the farmer, "but the load is just too heavy when it's bird and some."

So, whenever a load is very hard or even impossible to carry, think of John Harmony saying, "The load is just too heavy when it's bird and some," and you will remember the word

BURDENSOME

C

The Maudlin Movie House, in the mountain town of Tin Cup, was holding its annual contest to pick the saddest movie of the year. Producers and directors had come from Hollywood, Paris, Rome, and London. Critics from *The New York Times*, *The Wall Street Journal*, *The Washington Post*, and *The Tin Cup Gazette* had arrived, including the famous critic Scot Marco, who was to serve as judge.

Disliking mush, Scot had seen a thousand teary films and cried only nine times. To make Scot cry, a film had to be more than merely sad; it had to meet the highest teary standards.

Scot's job in Tin Cup was to view the year's saddest films and select winners for the Herbert P. Sniffle Tear-Jerker Awards. This year's competition included some blockbusters. One film from Russia featured a farmer who fell in love with his tractor, which broke his heart at harvest time by breaking down. From France came *The Fallen Soufflé* about a cook who lost his head because the queen disliked his dish. Another entry, from Poland, called *The Line*, described a woman who had waited in a food queue from Monday to Sunday. When she finally reached the front, she fainted dead away because seven days without food makes one weak. From Hollywood came sad films about people falling into volcanoes, disappearing into quicksand, slipping into glacial crevasses, and diving into swimming pools where the water was only a mirage.

Every day over dinner, directors and producers discussed camera angles and lighting; each afternoon over coffee, newspaper critics compared notes about acting performances; and all day long, Scot Marco watched film after film, trying to determine which one was the saddest. On the final night of the festival, the movie fans and experts gathered to learn the names of the winners.

The lights dimmed, a snare drum sounded a rat-a-tat-tat, and a woman dressed in red stepped out from behind the curtain to announce Scot Marco's decisions.

"Third place," she read from a card, "goes to *The Revenge of the Computers*. Although it didn't make Scot Marco cry, and thus didn't meet the highest teary standard, he selected it for its imaginative portrayal of technology ruining the world."

The audience clapped loudly.

"The second-place winner," she said, looking at the card, "is *Ice Cap Madness*. This film too didn't make Scot Marco cry, and thus didn't meet the highest teary standard, but he picked it for its realistic description of everyone drowning when the ice caps melt."

The audience cheered.

"The first prize," she announced, holding up the last card, "goes to *Little Em*, the story of a young girl put to work in the coal mines at the age of nine, run over by a truck at twelve, married at fourteen, divorced with a baby at fifteen, discovered for her singing voice at eighteen, made a millionairess at twenty-one, and killed in a plane crash at twenty-three."

The audience stood and yelled their approval.

"And the reason that *Little Em* has been awarded the first prize," she said, "is that this film, and only this film, was sad enough to make Scot Marco cry teary on."

So, whenever a standard or rule or test is used to judge something, think of *Little Em* winning first prize because the film was sad enough to make Scot Marco cry teary on, and you will remember the word

CRITERION

D

Emma Q. Late had spent all her life in New York City, doing the work that she did best: cleaning. She had scrubbed and waxed the floors at the Rockefeller Center. She had polished the display cases at Bloomingdale's and Macy's. She had brushed the velvet seats inside the theaters along Broadway. She had mopped the museums, scoured the subways, and vacuumed the airports. She had even hired a helicopter to fly past the face of the Statue of Liberty so she could wipe the statue's nose after a particularly long and heavy rain.

"A wet nose," declared Emma, "drips."

But for all Emma's efforts, New York remained a mess.

"Soot, and grime, and grease, and mud, and smoke, and streaks of spray paint on the sidewalks and the walls," she muttered crossly to herself. "When I was younger, I was glad for the variety. But now I'm getting old, and it's too much for me. If only I could specialize in dust."

Yes, that would be the life for Emma! She loved dustcloths, especially ones made of chamois. They were soft and smooth as suede, and quickly made a surface shiny. Feather dusters also pleased her, bushy like the tails of strutting peacocks and dyed such brilliant colors. And the dust itself! She loved the way it made her sneeze, with delicate achoos, three or four in a row. And she loved, when no one saw her, to move her index finger over dusty tabletops and draw her name with curlicues and flourishes, then wipe it all away with a swish of her cloth. So she left New York in search of some place far away, where lots of dust was waiting to be dusted.

"Where will you end up?" her friends all asked her.

So she went to Switzerland, having heard that in Geneva the lake glittered in the sun like diamonds. But the light glancing off the lake made the dust throughout the city dance so gaily in the sunbeams that Emma couldn't bear to clean it.

"Switzerland is swell," said Emma, "but not really the place that I set out to find. Maybe Finland will suit me." But in Scandinavia the winter sun shines for only an hour or two in the midafternoon, so that when Emma arrived, she could hardly see the dust to dust it.

"Finland is fantastic," said Emma, "but still not the place that I set out to find. I think I'll try Arabia."

Now Arabia was absolutely perfect. There

"I haven't the slightest idea," she said. "But when I find the place I'm looking for, I'll know it."

She stopped in London first, since she liked the rain and fancied fog as well. But rain and fog are not good friends of dust. In fact, they make dust rather damp so that it isn't dust at all. "London is lovely," said Emma, "but it isn't the place that I set out to find."

was dust on the minarets, dust in the ziggu-rats, and dust in the tents where the nomads all lived. And such lovely, dry dust! It gave Emma the chance to sneeze over and over. What's more, when she wrote her name on tabletops in Arabic, she could fashion far more curlicues and flourishes than she ever could in English. Emma set down her bags and unpacked.

"I'll never leave Arabia," she wrote to all her friends. "Finally, I have reached my dusty nation."

So, whenever someone arrives at the place that she set out to find, think of Emma, who traveled far and wide until at last she reached her dusty nation, and you will remember the word

DESTINATION

Sly Fox suspected Rhoda and Dendra of playing nasty tricks and blaming their sister, Honor.

First, there was the sneezing powder that someone had sprinkled on the teacher's bagel. Poor Mrs. Moffitt had sneezed for half a day, blaming Honor because an empty powder box was found in her schoolbag. But Sly Fox knew better. He had spoken with the manager of Tricks, Inc., a store that stocked sneezing powder. The manager remembered having sold a box of powder to two girls in purple dresses, a description that fit Rhoda and Dendra exactly.

Then someone had tampered with the playground swings. Several children landed in the middle of the duck pond when their swings fell apart. Honor was blamed because a screwdriver and a wrench were found in her bedroom. No one knew that Rhoda and Dendra had become friendly with the local auto mechanic. No one, that is, except old Sly Fox, who guessed that the mechanic had given the tools to Rhoda and Dendra.

So Sly Fox was ready when Rhoda and Dendra tried to trick him. The girls planned to exchange a pot of glue for a pot of honey in Sly Fox's pantry. "You watch for Sly while I make the switch," said Rhoda to Dendra. "If I wear a pair of Honor's shoes and leave footprints on his dirty kitchen floor, he'll think Honor was the thief."

But Sly caught them in his pantry.

"You're finished now," he said. "I'm too smart for you. I know every nasty thing you've done and how you've tried to blame it all on Honor. Come with me. I'm taking you to the police station."

Rhoda and Dendra begged Sly Fox to let them go.

"We'll do anything, anything you want," they cried.

"Then bake me a chocolate cake with hazelnut icing," Sly said.

"An extra big one," they shouted, "with your name written out in different-colored sprinkles."

"Just be sure it's here tomorrow morning," said Sly, "or it's off you go to the police."

Home ran the girls, and at midnight, when no one could see them, they went to the kitchen to bake Sly Fox's cake. But right before bedtime, Honor, terribly hungry, had made herself an omelet with every last egg in the kitchen. What were Rhoda and Dendra to do? The stores were all closed; no eggs meant no cake; no cake meant that Sly would turn them over to the police.

In the morning, they made their sorry way to Sly's house and begged him please to give them one more chance.

"Dear, kind Sly Fox," they cried, "believe us. We would have baked the chocolate cake, if only we had had the eggs. But Honor ate them all!"

"Eggs! Why should I believe that Honor ate your eggs?" growled Sly. "And even if she did, you blamed her for crimes that she didn't commit." And he marched the girls off to see Detective Dragnet, who was shocked to learn how Honor had been made to take the blame for Rhoda and Dendra's mischief. As punishment, he sentenced them to shine Honor's shoes for a year. Then, at a public meeting, he cleared Honor's name—a happy ending that came about only because of the eggs Honor ate.

So, whenever someone is accused of a crime and then shown to be innocent, think of the eggs Honor ate, and you will remember the word

EXONERATE

F

Though Titus Tooplumpski was the finest tailor in Petrograd, he was unhappy with his work. True, the city's noblemen came to him for their riding clothes and evening dress. But he wanted to be known for more than making seams look straight on Baron Bowlegs, or for building up the shoulders on the overcoats he made for General Runt. He longed for more creative ways to use his needles and his thread.

"Sewing pants just to hide the bulging belly of Lord Peter Paunch," thought Titus sadly, "is not what geniuses are meant to do. And I am a genius! It's time I stopped copying the fashions of the day and started creating some styles of my own."

So the next time General Runt ordered a frock coat, Titus Tooplumpski made one side of the coat longer than the other, and instead of designing the sleeves to stop right below the wrists, he ended one at the elbow and the second at the knees.

"Tooplumpski," fumed the general, "if you were in the cavalry, I'd have you trampled by horses. If you were in the infantry, I'd have you shot. As it is, I have half a mind to have you sewn inside a bear, with orders not to let you out until you've promised never, ever to make another coat like this one." And, turning on his heels, the general marched out of Titus's shop. Poor Titus. He remade the general's coat, giving him exactly what he wanted: something old-fashioned. The general was happy, but Titus was not.

"Genius," thought Titus, "is never appreciated in its own time. And yet maybe the general is right. Maybe clothing, instead of being pretty, should be useful." So Titus decided to sew something out of the ordinary, something fancy and yet practical. But what?

"I've got it!" cried Titus. "I know just what I can sew: an astronomer's walking suit for Baron Bowlegs."

The baron, you see, loved to look at the skies and keep track of the sun and the stars. So Titus made him a suit with a hat that could serve as a sundial, and a sleeve that could serve as a telescope, and a pant leg with lines that could serve as a graph.

"Clever, very clever," said the baron when he saw the suit that Titus had made. "You know, I think I rather like it."

Titus beamed with satisfaction.

"But tell me," said the baron, "could you add a leather strap across the shoulder, where I can hang my astrolabe? I use it to measure the height of the stars, and I never go gazing without it."

"Yes, of course," answered Titus.

"And what about hanging a pouch from the waist? I get hungry when I'm working," said the baron, "and I'd love to have a place to store some crackers and cheese."

"But of course," answered Titus.

"And what about a strip of fur right below my knees, all around the hem of the over-coat?" the baron asked.

"Anything you like," answered Titus, "but may I ask why? What's the purpose of fur on the hem?"

"Why, no purpose at all," laughed the baron, "except for decoration. To my mind, not everything has to be useful; and I think I'd rather like some fur below."

So, whenever you see a frill or a ruffle or any other decoration on a person's clothing, think of Baron Bowlegs saying, "I'd rather like some fur below," and you will remember the word

FURBELOW

G

In Samarkand there was a merchant, old and dying in his bed, and as he had no wife and one son only, he called him to his side to tell him of the treasure he had hidden in the leather trunk downstairs, in the black and twisted cellar that ran beneath their house.

The old man said that in the ancient days of Baghdad, when genies governed people's lives, a famous lamp built in the workshop of a wizard had passed into his family's hands. Strange and precious, the lamp held within its copper stomach three very different genies. But before the old man could say another word, his voice faltered, his eyes closed, and he passed from this world to the next.

Some weeks later, after his father had been laid to rest, Ahmad entered the dark cellar. Brushing aside the cobwebs, he made his way with a candle past several lifetimes of collected goods until he reached the hand-tooled leather trunk. Lifting up the lid, he could see in the candlelight garments made from silks and satin, bolts of Egyptian cotton, and rolls of pure white linen. Beneath these soft and lovely fabrics, he found the copper lamp.

That night, when the servants had all gone off to bed, Ahmad took the lamp and rubbed it slowly. The copper skin grew warm and radiant, glowing like a distant sun. The room, suddenly aglow, looked as if the morning light had risen in the east.

Without warning, from the lamp arose a round-faced, fat-bellied genie, licking his fingers and wiping his mouth with his sleeve.

"I am Genie Akbar," he announced, "and you've disturbed my evening meal. If you'd like a side of lamb with delicate herbs or a special lentil dish seasoned with ginger, then come along. Otherwise, just call me when you need me, and I'll bring you Genie-Akbar-Food. But please, don't interrupt me while I'm eating." Then he left.

Ahmad, determined to discover who the other genies were, rubbed the lamp again. In an instant, standing before him was a skinny, gray-faced man who looked as if he had no blood and who carried papyrus sheets with secret remedies for illness.

"I am Genie Abdullah," he said, "and unless you're sick, don't bother me. I'm a busy man. If you'd like a potion to cure the dropsy or a tincture to reduce a swelling, then I'll stay a bit. Otherwise, just call me when you need me, and I'll bring you Genie-Abdullah-Tonic. But please don't call unless you're really sick."

Then Abdullah turned and disappeared.

Anxious to meet the third genie, Ahmad again rubbed the magic lamp. Immediately there appeared a cheerful young man who smiled and laughed, extending his hand in friendship.

"I am Genie Ali," he announced, "and your wish is my command. As we are unacquainted, let us sit together now and drink a cup of tea, my favorite drink, so that we may get to know each other."

And they sat upon a silky couch, laughing happily as friends will do, sipping on their tea.

"Tell me," said Ahmad, "what is it that you bring?"

"I aim to please by being pleasant," said Genie Ali. "When you're sad, I'll bring you tea to make you cheerful."

"How very thoughtful," said Ahmad. "Whenever I need cheerfulness and kindness, I'll call for Genie-Ali-Tea."

So, whenever someone shows cheerfulness and kindness, think of Ali saying, "Genie-Ali-Tea," and you will remember the word

GENIALITY

H In the mountains, heavy snows began to fall. It was nearly time for the bears to sleep away the winter months. Some used the old miners' shacks and mines, abandoned years ago when all the gold ran out; some snuggled up in an old log; some dug holes under trees and covered themselves with leaves and branches. Sleeping through the winter came naturally to all the bears—except Nathaniel.

Nate, as he was called, had moved to California from Canada, where the winter cold made bones brittle and broke the beaks of birds. Sleeping through the winter made lots of sense in Canada, but in California, which has a milder climate, Nate couldn't understand why the bears didn't spend the winter sporting in the snow. You see, Nate was very active.

In fact, Nate never stopped moving. He was a dynamo, a hurricane, a cyclone, and a whirlwind all wrapped up in one. Each morning, as soon as there was light, he raced from one end of the snowy valley to the other, waking up the other bears, reminding them that to keep mind and body healthy, they had to exercise. Then he quickly performed a hundred jumping jacks to make his point. In a flash he was off to organize snowball fights, igloo-building contests, nature hikes, and mountain climbing expeditions. He

30

invited the other bears to join him for a swim upstream against the icy river current. He said that swimming downstream with the current was for sissies.

"This guy's hyper," said one bear.

"He never stops," remarked a second.

"I'm ready for a long rest and honey dreams," sighed a third.

Exhausted from their play, they eagerly looked forward to a long and blissful winter's sleep. But Nate had other plans.

"The snow's now covered all the mountain rocks," he pointed out. "The hills are deep with powder. It's time to make some skis. And while we're at it, we can cut some branches for snow-shoes and some boards for toboggans."

"When do we start our winter sleep?" the bears asked one another.

"Sleep?" said a brown bear sarcastically, "Nate never sleeps."

"He's hyper," said a grizzly.

Nate paid no attention. "Why don't we whittle some wooden runners," he suggested, "so we can skate on frozen mountain lakes?"

"What about our winter sleep?" complained the elder bears.

"What about our rest and honey dreams?" grumbled the younger bears. "Just because you're hyper doesn't mean we all are!"

Nate couldn't believe his ears. But what could he do? The bears refused to be convinced. They loved their lazy ways, and Nate could see it was impossible to change them.

"Winter is a wonderland you really shouldn't miss," he said. "But if it's winter sleep you want, then I suggest you do the opposite from me, hyper Nate."

So, whenever animals sleep through the winter, think of Nate telling the other bears to act "the opposite from me, hyper Nate," and you will remember the word

HIBERNATE

I

The fairies and imps of Hemming Way were tired of being bullied by Brutus. As a youth, Brutus had been a courteous bull. But now that he was grown, he was a meanie. What had happened to him?

"If you ask me," said Patsy Pixie, "he's simply too big for his britches."

"What he's too big for," replied Ira Imp, "is his blankie."

Yes, Brutus had a blankie, which he dearly loved. It had come from Spain, and on a hot summer's day, he would snuggle up with his blankie to dream away the afternoon. At night, of course, he took his blankie to bed—and again settled into wonderful dreams.

Sadly, though, Brutus's dreams led him astray. According to Ira, no sooner did Brutus fall asleep than he imagined himself in a bull-ring, rushing at a toreador's red cloth with such daring and speed that the sword never touched him. Again and again, he would charge at the cloth until the toreador passed out from exhaustion. Then Brutus would march in triumph through the village, garlands of flowers hung round his neck.

"You're nuts," Sylvan Sylph said to Ira. "Brutus would never dream up such stuff. And anyway, how would you know if he did?"

"I know," answered Ira, "because only

yesterday I snatched that very dream from his head. Imps can do that sort of thing, you know."

"Nonsense," said Felicity Fairy. "The mind's a private place."

"This is no time for a lesson in life," sighed Ira. "We've got to get that blankie away from him. I suggest that we steal it."

"Stealing is wrong," said Felicity, "even if the blankie does make Brutus misbehave."

"True," admitted Ira, "but we'll give it back to him if he promises to be good."

"There is no way," said Sylvan, "that tiny folk like us could ever steal a prized possession from a bull the size of Brutus."

"Wanna bet?" replied Ira. "With some help from my friends, I'll steal it myself."

"Impossible," said Felicity. "Remember, every afternoon when the sun is at its height, and every evening when the sun's about to set, Brutus lies down on top of his blankie—all two tons of him."

"That may be," said Ira, "but the sun also rises. And my name's not Ira Imp of Hemming Way if, first thing tomorrow morning, I don't nab his blankie."

At dawn, under Ira's direction, the fairies and the sylphs fluttered through the pasture, wearing skirts of rose petals that looked exactly like a red cloth waving in the wind. When they were close enough to Brutus to be seen, but still far enough away to be safe, Ira woke up Brutus by ringing a bell in his ear. Brutus opened one eye, caught sight of the rose-petal skirts, and charged, leaving the blankie behind. Quick as a flash, Ira grabbed the blankie in both hands and flew off.

"Well, I'll be," exclaimed Sylvan in utter amazement. "It may have been highly unlikely, but I've actually seen an imp rob a bull."

So, whenever something highly unlikely happens, think of Sylvan's amazement at seeing an imp rob a bull, and you will remember the word

IMPROBABLE

J

Wally Woeful never smiled. Each day, with a sorrowful face, he shuffled along the path from his mountain cabin to the glittering river in the valley below, where he sifted the sands for droplets of gold. Up and down the river he went looking for nuggets, bitterly complaining that once he had come close to being a very rich man.

"Oh, it wasn't panning gold that almost made me rich," he said. "I nearly made a fortune working in the city, until a gold-digging buzzard ruined me."

Bearded and bent in the back, he followed the river, combing the pebbles and crying to one and all that his best friend, Jerry, had stolen his only true treasure. Day in and day out, for ten years,

Wally wailed about his having been cheated out of a fortune by someone named Jerry. Finally, the other miners had had enough.

"All we hear is Jerry this and Jerry that," one miner grumbled.

"The weeping and wailing around here," complained a second, "is enough to give a mountain lion a headache."

"I don't even believe there is such a person as this Jerry fellow," said a third miner, "but if there is, I want to hear about him. What exactly did he do?"

The time had finally come for Wally Woeful to tell his story—not to cry and yell and howl, if he could help it, not to make a bitter fuss again about his old friend Jerry, but just to tell his tale. Wally promised he would try to be calm.

His story was a simple one. He had gone to college and had studied business. He hoped one day to strike it rich. After leaving school, he took a job at an advertising agency, writing ads, all types of ads: car ads, food ads, travel ads, and even ads for a large newspaper, the *Times*.

Then one day, the man who owned the advertising agency where Jerry worked said that the *Times* needed a new and special ad, a catchy phrase that people would remember. A good ad, he explained, was like a vein of gold, a nugget to treasure. And if anyone came up with such an ad, that person, he promised, would be made a vice president of the company, with a sky-high salary.

Suddenly, Wally howled, "Jerry stole my ad!" The other miners told him to settle down and continue with his story.

"Well," Wally sniffled, "it was a Friday afternoon. Jerry came to my office. He said his own ad did not pan out. He asked if he could look at mine. He was my best friend, so I showed it to him."

Wally then began to moan, thinking of his loss.

"What did the ad say?" asked one of the miners.

"I had written, 'buy the *Times* because it has an eye for a lie and a tooth for the truth.'"

No sooner had he said this than Wally began to wail, asking over and over again how Jerry, his best friend, could have stolen his ad, become vice president instead of him, and then given poor Wally the boot. "Jerry, it was mine," he cried. "My ad, Jerry!"

Bursting into tears, he let out one final, "Jerry, my ad!"

So, whenever someone tells a tearful tale or makes a sad complaint, think of Wally crying, "Jerry, my ad," and you will remember the word

JEREMIAD

K

Joanna and Daniel Grant had never had a pet. Their father didn't want one; he said that pets were just a nuisance. Their mother, who was far more sympathetic than her husband, suggested that an aquarium would brighten up the house.

"You can't hold a fish or cuddle up to it," said Joanna.

So Mrs. Grant suggested that they buy a singing bird.

"The same problem," said Daniel, "and they toss their birdseed everywhere."

Mrs. Grant had hoped to steer the children to a little pet, one that wouldn't take much care.

"We want something out of the ordinary," explained Joanna, "like an anteater."

"Forget it!" said their father. Their mother suggested that the children ask their science teacher what kind of unusual pet could be kept without a lot of fuss.

The next day, Joanna and Daniel ran into the garden, where Mrs. Grant was pruning roses, and told her which one they had chosen.

"A boa constrictor," announced Daniel.

"They're very gentle and easy to take care of," added Joanna. "That's what our teacher told us."

So Mrs. Grant took the children to the pet shop, where they bought a young boa constrictor, which they called Julius Squeezer.

Julius lived in a cage, but the children often let him curl around their arms or legs while they were in the house. In no time at all, Julius grew too large for the cage and began to crawl from room to room.

One evening, while

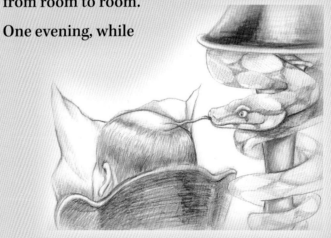

Mr. Grant was reading his paper, Julius slithered up the pole lamp and dropped down on his head. What a storm that created! Worse, a few days later, Julius was found in the dryer and then in the clothes basket. But the worst was yet to come. One night, Mr. Grant climbed into bed and found lying next to him Julius Squeezer. The next morning, Julius went back to the pet shop. Joanna and Daniel cried to have another pet.

"How about two cats?" he asked. "One for each of you? Cats are cuddly and furry and have beautiful eyes. They make wonderful pets; they play with string and with balls; and they aren't any trouble."

The children agreed, so they and their mom again marched to the pet store, where they purchased two little cats, Beatrice and Benedict. All day long the cats rolled on the floor pawing sunbeams, or wrestling, or chasing their tails. Joanna and Daniel held them on their laps and let them sleep at the foot of their beds.

Everyone was happy until Beatrice and Benedict climbed on the kitchen counter, knocked over the jellies and jams, rolled around in the sticky stuff, and raced through the house, brushing up against the furniture, staining the rugs, and soiling the linens and towels.

"That's it!" exploded Mr. Grant. "No more pets in this house!"

"It was just an accident," cried the children, hoping to keep Beatrice and Benedict from being returned to the pet shop. "Cats are usually no trouble."

"You say cats are usually no trouble," grumbled Mr. Grant, "but I say cats in jam are."

So, whenever something is confusing and funny and noisy, think of Mr. Grant saying, "You say cats are usually no trouble, but I say cats in jam are," and you will remember the word

KATZENJAMMER

L

Bossy the Cow had mysteriously lost her energy. After years of giving orders to the farmyard animals, she no longer demanded that the rooster lend his comb to the shaggy old goat, no longer insisted that the sheep give up woolgathering, and no longer advised the piglets to eat from a plate with a fork and a spoon. She just sat on her haunches and left everyone alone, saying only "day's ease."

The farmyard animals were grateful to be free of Bossy's nagging, but they also worried that she might be ill. After a while, they actually started to miss her old behavior. They could see that she just wasn't Bossy unless she gave orders.

Even at the risk of being nagged from morn to midnight, they wanted their old Bossy back.

"What do you imagine could be wrong with her?" the rooster asked the hen. "And what could she mean by 'day's ease?'"

"I wouldn't be surprised," answered Henny, "if Bossy is simply relaxing because she knows that she's about to lay an egg."

"Hee-haw," brayed the donkey, "that's an awfully foolish idea."

"Well, I never!" humphed Henny, highly offended. "I haven't heard *you* coming up with a better explanation."

"All I can say," brayed the donkey, "is this: you ought to ask Bossy what's causing her apathy."

"Her what?" said the rooster; but the donkey was already heading back to his barn stall, where he spent his lazy hours reading through a dictionary. He had just reached the word apathy.

"What he means," said the owl, who was listening in, "is that you ought to ask Bossy why she doesn't give a hoot about anything."

"Thanks," said the rooster, "but it isn't polite to eavesdrop."

"It's lucky for you that I did," said the owl, "since you didn't understand the donkey without me." The owl then fell asleep.

Having no one to talk to, the rooster strutted down to the green and golden pasture where Bossy was quietly daydreaming. What a sight she was! She had been sleeping in the grass so long that a spider had woven a cobweb from her ear to her hoof.

"Bossy, what's the matter?" asked the rooster. "What's become of all your old pizzazz?"

"Day's ease," moaned the cow to the rooster's confusion, "day's ease."

"I don't understand!" cried the rooster. "You've had day after day of day's ease for a month. How much day's ease do you need?"

"Not day's *ease*," Bossy answered very slowly, "daisies."

"Oh my goodness," cried the rooster.

And without another word, the rooster flew across the pasture to a field of daisies where Bossy once grazed, but where a fence now kept her out. Jumping over the fence, the rooster plucked a dozen daisies and then raced them back to Bossy, who ate them at once.

"Oh wonders!" she sighed, "you saved me! I never realized till I lost my daisy patch . . . but I seem to have no energy unless I eat at least one daisy every day. Isn't it strange?"

"I've never heard anything like it!" the rooster replied. "But now that I know, I'll be sure to bring you daisies every morning for breakfast. I'd rather have you bossing me and all the others, too, than to have you lose your energy and end up being lack-a-daisy-cow."

So, whenever someone is lacking in energy or interest, think of how Bossy lolled about when she was lack-a-daisy-cow, and you will remember the word

LACKADAISICAL

When Professor Horatio Cavendish wasn't teaching English to the boys—really, the brats—at the Middle Berry School in the country west of Nowhither, he would hide in the river reeds or in the tall field grass, staring through his binoculars hoping to see marvelous birds. Rarely was he disappointed, for most of the birds of the world passed directly through Nowhither on their flight to wherever. And Professor Cavendish had seen most of them: towhees and shrikes, puffins and pewits, grackles and hoopoes, coots and loons, dippers and boobies and kittiwakes. But much to his sorrow, he'd never seen the rarest of songbirds: the ruffled humdinger.

After waiting thirty years, he'd begun to think that he'd never see one. He grew fretful. And the brats of the Middle Berry School, aware of Professor Cavendish's frustration, did their best to make him lose his temper. Why? Because they found it quite hilarious to hear him say, as he always did when he was angry, "Fie on it!"

So the boys would deliberately kick a soccer ball through the professor's open window. One time it hit the metal wastebasket and made an awful clatter. Another time it scattered a pile of tests all over the classroom. Once it even bounced off the head of Professor Cavendish himself. While the boys laughed, the professor would seize the ball, throw it out the window, and angrily yell, "Fie on it!"

In the classroom, the boys were no better behaved. When they were asked to write a paper describing where they lived, someone was sure to make a copy of the Gettysburg Address, saying he'd forgotten his own address and therefore had borrowed Lincoln's.

Professor Cavendish would give the paper an F, throw it on the floor, and, as the boys howled with delight, holler, "Fie on it!"

Every day the boys annoyed Professor Cavendish so that he'd say, "Fie on it!" They called the poet Henry Wadsworth Longfellow, Shortfellow; and the professor would pound the desk and cry, "Fie on it!" They would call

the poem "Evangeline," "Evangelist"; and the professor would stamp his foot and yell, "Fie on it!" They would talk about Hiawatha in the Forest of Gumee Gitche, and the professor would tear his hair and cry, "Fie on it! Not Gumee Gitche! Gitche Gumee!" And so it went: the brats making mistakes and Professor Cavendish never missing the chance to say, "Fie on it!"

But one day, when the boys were particularly bratty, a ruffled humdinger settled on the classroom windowsill. At first the professor didn't notice. He was busy asking the class which character in Shakespeare had divided his kingdom among his three daughters. But just as the brats called out "King Fear," the ruffled humdinger broke into song. Professor Cavendish stood still as a statue, staring in amazement at the humdinger. It was the bird for which he'd waited thirty years! Professor Horatio Cavendish smiled a warmer smile than he had ever smiled before. And because he was so happy, he completely forgot to say, "Fie on it."

As a result, the boys were confused. Wasn't the character's name King Lear? Or was it? Maybe the king was King Fear after all. The boys were too puzzled to know what was right—and all because their teacher missed a fie.

So, whenever someone confuses or puzzles another person, think of Professor Horatio Cavendish, who missed a fie, and you will remember the word

N

Born in Scotland, Mr. and Mrs. McPoodle wore tams, played bagpipes, and said aye for yes and nay for no. They also explored deep underground caverns. People who engage in this sport are called cavers or spelunkers. Wearing helmets with electric lights, they find openings in the ground that lead to rooms and passageways formed by underground rivers. In this black wilderness, they look for stalactites, which hang from the cave ceilings and resemble jeweled icicles, and for stalagmites, which form cones on cave floors from the dripping water.

Having explored all the deep caves in Scotland, the McPoodles decided to go spelunking in the Missouri Ozarks, which have more than four thousand caverns. As they made their way through the thick woods and rocky hills, they saw a gurgling stream that seemed to disappear in a hole. Peering over the lip, they discovered a pit that dropped away into cold darkness. Mrs. McPoodle excitedly said, "Let's explore!" From their backpacks they removed all their gear. For warmth, they dressed in woolen long johns, jeans, overalls, sweaters, parkas, and leather work boots. For safety and light, they each wore a helmet with an electric lamp. For emergencies, they carried pocketknives, water bottles, and food.

Tying their rope to a tree, they slid down into the hole. Mr. McPoodle went first, just in case danger lay ahead. About a hundred feet

down, they reached a room with towering columns and a needled ceiling of stalactites. Out of the mud and sticky clay floor rose stalagmites shaped like Christmas trees, stools, posts, and even totem poles. Below this room, in the inky darkness, they could hear a river. Mrs. McPoodle said, "Let's descend till we see it." Mr. McPoodle agreed, saying, "Aye, dear."

With a second rope, they climbed down until the light on their helmets lit up a blue lake. In the quiet, glassy underground water, they watched the ghostly dartings of blind fish and saw the dark eyes of bright orange-and-black cave salamanders. Next to the lake they found numerous bones of ice age animals like jaguars and saber-toothed cats and American lions. Off to one side, Mrs. McPoodle noticed a small passageway. "Let's keep exploring," she said. Mr. McPoodle agreed again, saying, "Aye, dear." And so they continued their downward journey into the depths of the earth.

Suddenly they heard a deafening roar: the sound of a thundering waterfall. Moving closer, they were nearly knocked down by the noise because the cave magnified the sound. The icy spray from the water made them feel cold and clammy. They heard a gentle flutter, followed by the piercing cry that bats use to find their way in the darkness. "The waterfall is beautiful," shouted Mr. McPoodle over the noise, "but it's getting spooky. I think we ought to start climbing back to the surface. In any case, best as I can tell, we have reached the bottom."

"You mean," said Mrs. McPoodle, "we can't go any lower?"

He shook his head. "Nay, dear."

So, whenever someone (or something) reaches the lowest point, think of Mr. McPoodle saying, "Nay, dear," and you will remember the word

NADIR

Detective Douglas D. Duffy of Scotland Yard was having no luck. His man couldn't figure out who had robbed the P. T. Blarney Circus.

"Let's go over what we know again," he said to his assistants, Dingle and Dougal.

"Well," began Dingle, "the safe that held the payroll was in the trailer by the big top."

"And," added Dougal, "it was guarded day and night by two huge dogs, ferocious as lions. That's all we know."

"That's all!" fumed Detective Duffy. "What kind of detectives are you? I can see it's time to call in my mother."

As soon as Mrs. Duffy arrived, she set down her bags and said, "Just leave everything to me. That way things will turn out best. I'll solve this case within the hour."

"Begging your pardon, ma'am," Dingle and Dougal blurted out together, "but if we're all

stumped by this case, how can you—"

"Now listen here, you young whippersnappers," interrupted Mrs. Duffy, "there isn't a mystery I can't solve. When Douglas was a boy and all the locks in our neighborhood were being picked, I knew the culprit was the locksmith. And when Douglas was a teenager, there was the case of the poison pen letters. I solved that one by sending Douglas through the city with phony petitions to gather up handwriting samples! So unless you have any objections"—as naturally Dingle and Dougal did not—"let's hear about this investigation."

The two men explained that they had questioned the fat lady because, the day after the theft, she bought herself a motorcycle. But the fat lady had bank receipts to prove that she'd been saving for months. Next they questioned the snake charmer, who had scared them half to death with a cobra round one arm and a python round the other. Dingle and Dougal felt sure he was guilty because the day after the theft he showed up at the circus with a diamond the size of a fist. But it turned out his aunt had died the night before and given him the diamond, and he had a copy of her will to prove his story. They also questioned the sword swallower because of his new silver sword.

"And we didn't find it easy," added Dougal, "what with the way he was constantly clearing his throat."

"But we discovered," said Detective Duffy, "that the silver sword was not really silver. It was just painted that color."

"Tell me," said Mrs. Duffy, "why are those two huge dogs tied up outside the trailer near the big top?"

"They were guarding the safe where the

payroll was held," said Detective Duffy. "We still can't imagine how anyone got past them."

"Case solved!" cried Mrs. Duffy. "Call in the lion tamer!"

In he roared, carrying his whip in one hand and a chair in the other. Mrs. Duffy looked him over and said, "Fess up, young fellow. Or I'll spank you."

"Please not that," trembled the lion tamer. "I confess I stole the payroll from the safe. But how did you know?"

"Why, who else besides a lion tamer could have managed those ferocious dogs?" explained Mrs. Duffy.

"See, boys," said Detective Duffy to Dingle and Dougal. "Didn't I tell you? Things are always best when left up to Mom!"

So, whenever something is the best that it can be, think of Detective Duffy saying, "Things are always best when left up to Mom," and you will remember the word

OPTIMUM

P

Each year at the Amboseli Wildlife Park in Kenya, Africa, the animals met to elect a leader. The election always caused a fuss because each group of animals wanted one of their own to be chosen. As usual, the lions were behaving like bullies.

"We are kings of the beasts," they roared, "and therefore the boss ought to be a lion."

"Pipe down!" cried the water buffaloes. "We all know how lazy you are, sleeping twenty hours a day."

When the lions bared their teeth, the water buffaloes silenced them by saying, "We're bigger, meaner, and tougher than you. The boss should be a water buffalo, because even the rhinos run from us."

"Who said?" bellowed the rhinos. "We have the toughest skin of all. That's why a rhino

deserves to be boss."

"You may have the toughest skin," said the cobras, "but you're nearly blind and we have the strongest poison."

"Look who's talking about being blind," said the birds. "You can hardly see more than a few feet in front of you. But we can soar above the ground and view the whole world."

"You're weaklings," barked the boar.

"Yes," answered the birds, "but we're the fastest animals of all. We can fly; can you?"

Pretty soon a terrible argument ensued, with the gazelles insisting they were the most beautiful; the elephants proclaiming they were the strongest; the giraffes saying they were the most graceful; and the leopards snarling they were the best hunters.

On and on they argued until Ann, a park ranger, drove up in her yellow jeep. In times of famine and drought, Ann fed and watered the animals. She cured the sick and chased poachers from the park. All the animals loved her. So when she spoke, everyone listened.

"What's the trouble here?" she asked.

Willy the fox explained that each group of animals wanted the boss to be chosen from their group.

"What about the fishes?" she asked.

"They're not animals," answered the coyotes.

"Precisely!" said Ann. And, pointing to a little stream running through the salt marshes where the animals had gathered, she said, "Right here, under your noses, is where the golden fishes swim."

Hearing Ann's voice, the fishes surfaced from the stream and asked if one of them could be boss, since no fish had ever been elected before. The other animals howled with laughter.

"Since you can't decide politely among yourselves," said Ann, "I will pick the group that hasn't misbehaved: the fishes."

The other animals, out of respect for Ann, remained quiet as a stone. Then one golden fish yelled, "Hip-hip-hooray! She's on our side! The one who took our part is Ann."

So, whenever someone takes another's part or side, think of the golden fish saying, "The one who took our part is Ann," and you will remember the word

PARTISAN

The Quimbilian spaceship Starlight, heading home from a scientific mission to the forty-fourth galaxy, was forced to land on planet earth so Captain Domanda, who had broken his wrist while exploring a black hole, could find a doctor. Most everything else about the Quimbilians was perfectly human; they could even speak English. But all Quimbilian wrists were made of springs and hinges. They were so complicated that to be repaired they required a doctor with a knowledge of engineering.

Slowing down to 55 ly/p/h (light years per hour), the spaceship reached the planet earth within a day and landed in the little town of Snugville. There, Captain Domanda found the hospital and entered the emergency room, where a short, roly-poly man introduced himself as Dr. Malatesta.

"That's quite a wrist," said the doctor.

"Queer construction."

"How is it different from yours?" asked Captain Domanda.

Dr. Malatesta rolled up his shirt sleeves and held out his wrists in front of him for the captain to see.

"How do they work?" asked Captain Domanda. "Are they very strong? Can you bend them back so that your fingers touch your arm? Do they need to be oiled?"

Dr. Malatesta spent an hour explaining the human wrist and how it works. Then, because he knew a lot about mechanics, he repaired Captain Domanda's wrist of springs and hinges.

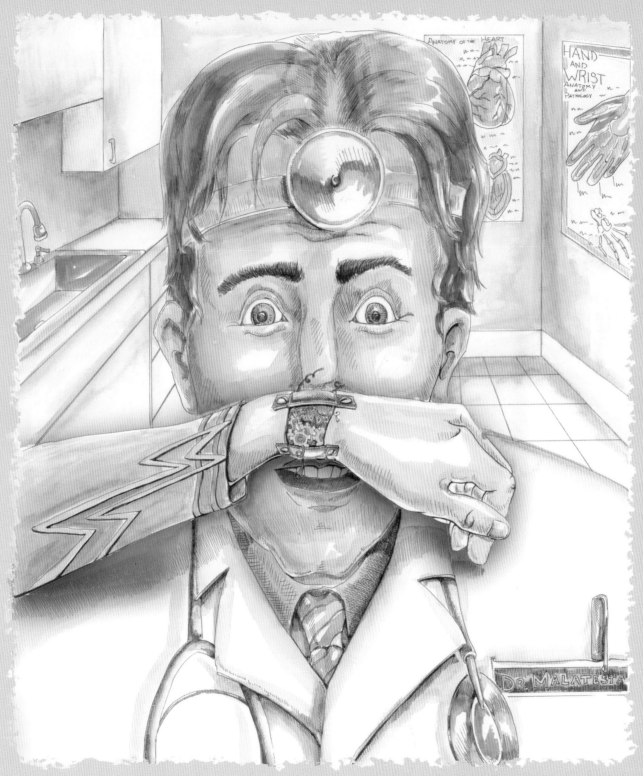

61

Captain Domanda thanked him, paid the bill, and left the hospital. But before returning to his spaceship, he decided to do some sightseeing.

Everywhere he went, he asked questions. In the supermarket, he said, "What's this?" holding up a bunch of carrots; "or this?" holding up a box of frozen shrimp; "or this?" holding up a can of coffee. In the television store, he asked, "How does it work? How often does a person watch it? Does it help children with their schoolwork?" In the video arcade, he asked, "How much money does it cost to play? Do you win anything? What's the point?"

Not for one moment did he stop asking questions. He wanted to know why some people drive new cars and some old ones; why some people dress in good clothes and others in shabby clothes; why some people live in lovely houses and some in hovels.

At the end of the day, he returned to his spaceship and left for Quimbilia. The people in the town were amazed. Never had they heard anyone ask so many questions.

"We should have asked his name," said the grocer.

"We didn't have a chance," said the hospital nurse, "because he never stopped asking questions."

"Then let me suggest," said Dr. Malatesta, thinking of the hinges and the springs he'd repaired, "that we give him the name Queer Wrist."

So, whenever someone asks question after question, think of Dr. Malatesta suggesting that "we give him the name Queer Wrist," and you will remember the word

QUERIST

R

George and Gertie Gothic lived in a lovely old house. The floors, made from hand-cut planks of oak and rubbed with homemade wax, shone like gold. Two stone fireplaces, one upstairs and one down, blazed all winter long. Indian gourds hung from the ceiling, and comforters filled with goose feathers covered the beds. On the front porch, a wooden swing rocked gently in the breeze. Circling the house was a metal fence attached to a rusty, squeaky gate. In the garden, lilacs grew, and also wild roses, grapes, and honeysuckle.

Nothing pleased Mr. Gothic so much as coming home each evening, hearing the squeak of the gate as he opened it, and calling to his wife, "I'm here!" For her part, Mrs. Gothic, an artist, took endless pleasure in painting what she saw from her window:

the far hills, her garden, the flowers, and the squeaky gate, all brown with rust.

But the quiet country life of the Gothics suddenly came to an end when George's company transferred him to a large and busy city, and bought the Gothics a newly furnished modern house, with shiny kitchen cabinets, a microwave oven, refrigerator, freezer, garbage compressor and disposal, dishwasher, clothes dryer, and washing machine. The house also

came with air-conditioning, indirect lighting, forced-air heating, wall-to-wall stain-free carpets, TV sets and telephones upstairs and down, a built-in stereo system, walk-in closets, three bathrooms, a sauna, and a home computer. The furniture was made from stainless steel and canvas and leather strips. In fact, all the rooms, with their modern furnishings and white walls, made the house look futuristic.

"I feel as if I'm living in a plastic cup," complained Mr. Gothic, "a plastic cup filled with electrical gadgets. I miss the country."

"You'll see," Mrs. Gothic consoled him, "how different you'll feel once our old furniture arrives."

But still Mr. Gothic complained. "I feel the absence of the country . . . the old familiar landmarks."

Mrs. Gothic pointed out that the city was not the country and that a modern house was not a farmhouse.

"It's not just the city or the house," explained Mr. Gothic, "it's the little things I miss, the country touches right outside my door. For example, I miss our metal fence."

So Mrs. Gothic had one made for their small garden. She also planted lilacs, wild roses, grapes, and honeysuckle.

"It's beginning to feel more like the country," he said, "but something's still missing."

"We have the flowers and the bushes, and a new fence," said Mrs. Gothic, "with a new gate . . ."

"That's it!" said Mr. Gothic. "I know what we need to make our city house feel like the country."

"What's that?" asked Mrs. Gothic.

"A rusty gate!"

So, whenever someone lives or stays in the country, think of Mr. Gothic asking for "a rusty gate," and you will remember the word

RUSTICATE

S

Sammy Splinterstein was as thin as a hummingbird's rib. His face resembled the edge of a knife. He was so skinny that when he turned his body sideways, he looked like a twig with an apple on top.

Mrs. Splinterstein had tried everything to help him put on weight. She fed him creams and cakes and jams. She made him food with butter, oil, and fat. She served him rich casseroles and pastas, marbled steaks, and gooey pastries. But nothing seemed to help. When he stepped upon a scale, the needle hardly rose at all. He was but the shadow of a man.

Not knowing what else to do, Mrs. Splinterstein went to the weight clinic and asked Dr. Nostrum for his advice.

Looking through his potions and prescriptions, the doctor shook his head and explained, "All the pills and medicines that I have on my shelf are to help fat people lose weight. I have nothing to help skinny people gain weight."

Mrs. Splinterstein was terribly discouraged. But then she remembered her Aunt Obie East, who weighed a couple hundred pounds. Now Aunt Obie East was a woman of very few words. In fact, she hardly spoke at all because she was too busy eating. So when

Mrs. Splinterstein asked her what she recommended for putting on weight, she answered with one word: "Syrup!"

"You mean," asked Mrs. Splinterstein, "I should put rivers of syrup on Sammy's waffles and pancakes?"

Aunt Obie East, who was munching on a lamb chop, said "Mm-hmm" and went on eating.

The next morning, Mrs. Splinterstein put in front of Sam a heaping plate of pancakes, smothered in syrup.

"I hate syrup!" complained Mr. Splinterstein. "Get this awful stuff away from me."

Mrs. Splinterstein was terribly upset. But then it occurred to her that she could succeed if she put syrup in Sam's food secretly. From that meal on, she included syrup in all his dishes: in the Hungarian goulash, in the pot roast, in the lamb stew, in the fish broth, in the chicken gumbo. She mixed it in his vegetables and hid it between the layers of his lasagna. But so secretive and careful was she that Mr. Splinterstein never once detected in his food a single trace of syrup.

At first the weight that he put on was hardly noticeable. But in six months he no longer looked like a skeleton with a hatchet face. After a year, he could hardly believe his eyes. In the mirror he saw standing in front of him not Frankenstein, but Sammy Splinterstein.

"How in the world," asked Mr. Splinterstein, "did you manage to fatten me up?"

"Secretly," answered Mrs. Splinterstein. "I've secretly been adding something to all your dishes."

"You did it," said Mr. Splinterstein in amazement, "by means of secret dishes?"

"Actually," replied Mrs. Splinterstein, "by means of syrup dishes."

So, whenever someone acts secretively, think of Mrs. Splinterstein saying, "by means of syrup dishes," and you will remember the word

SURREPTITIOUS

T

Business was so slow at the Snoresville Department Store that the salespeople took turns sneaking into the dressing rooms, where they could catch a little snooze. As a result, no one was awake when a customer came to buy. The manager was frantic. Business would never improve if the employees continued to sleep on the job. He therefore demanded that everyone stay awake or else risk being fired.

Talk about change! Over at perfumes, the saleswomen tucked vials of smelling salts under their sleeves to snap them back to life when they began to doze. In the furniture department, they installed

bells to go off every ten minutes. In sportswear, they bought a dog that would snap at their feet if they fell asleep. Every department changed except one: the tie department.

Timmy the tie salesman was too lazy to make any changes. But he also didn't want to lose his job. How dare the others improve their departments, while his remained shabby? He'd make them all sorry. Yes, that's what he'd do, not by making his own department better, but by ruining everyone else's.

So Timmy marched through the store, making trouble wherever he went. He put hundreds of moths in

the sweater department so that the turtle-necks and cardigans and crewnecks ended up all full of holes. In the women's department, he dumped itching powder into the dresses and into the skirts and the blouses, too. He clipped the arms off the suits in the men's department and jumped on the sofas and chairs in the furniture department till the springs sprang out of the cushions. He even set a skunk running round the perfumes, with the stinky result that the counter was closed for two weeks till the smell went away.

The sales staff was furious. "Fire him!" they cried.

"I would love to," the manager replied, "but he's the store owner's cousin."

The other departments decided that something had to be done. "Look at how much trouble Timmy's caused us with his raids," they said. "The time has come for us to pay him back. Tomorrow, bright and early, we will raid his racks of ties."

At seven in the morning, before the store had opened, they gathered at the tie counter and started their destruction. They cut some of the ties into ribbons. They dribbled ketchup and juice on the others. Then they draped the damaged ties across the counter.

Timmy, who hadn't suspected a thing, was enraged when he discovered the damage. He called the staff together to scold them for their nastiness. But the others only laughed to see the way he carried on. Who was he to lecture them? They were glad they had raided his department.

"It worked," they laughed. "Listen to him scold! Listen to him lecture! We really did produce a tie raid."

So, whenever someone angrily lectures or scolds, think of Timmy's colleagues saying, "We really did produce a tie raid," and you will remember the word

TIRADE

U

Priscilla Piglet, age seven, never told a lie. So she was naturally nervous when she went to visit her Aunt Dagmar, who wrote children's books and made up stories.

"Did you know," said Priscilla, "if you tell a lie, your nose will grow?"

"Sometimes," answered Aunt Dagmar mysteriously, "the choice is between telling a lie or being attacked by the wolf."

Aunt Dagmar lived in a stone house deep in the woods, where her life passed quietly, except for those times when Wintergreen Wolf came knocking at her door. "Dagmar!" he would call. "I'm all dressed up with no place to go. What do you say the two of us go dancing?"

With the figure and face of a movie star and the brains of a professor, Dagmar Piglet was a knockout. But she had no interest in being pawed and devoured by Wintergreen Wolf.

"Aren't you afraid," asked her niece Priscilla, "that the wolf will sneak up on you while you're walking in the woods?"

Aunt Dagmar smiled. "That klutz? You can hear him a mile away as he clomps through the forest kicking pine cones and whistling 'Dixie.' Now how about a cup of tea and a biscuit?" But just as Aunt Dagmar raised the teapot to pour, a great clamor arose outside.

Wintergreen Wolf stood outside the house thumping a tub and bellowing, "Dagmar, I'm all dressed up with no place to go. Open the door and I'll take you dancing."

Aunt Dagmar told him, "Scram!"

"Open the door," coughed Wintergreen Wolf, "or I'll huff and I'll puff and I'll blow your house down."

"Wintergreen," said Aunt Dagmar, "your lungs are so bad from smoking you couldn't blow out a match."

Of course, Aunt Dagmar was right. Wintergreen thought it made him look big and tough to smoke. But, in fact, it hurt his breathing, stained his fingers and teeth, and fouled his breath.

"Open the door," yelled the wolf, "or I'll burn your house down!"

Aunt Dagmar laughed. "No chance. This house is made of stone."

"Open the door," said Wintergreen, "or I'll stand here forever."

"If you want to enter a woman's house," said Aunt Dagmar, "I'll tell you just how to do it."

Priscilla Piglet could hardly believe her ears.

"What you need to do," advised Aunt Dagmar, "is get a college degree. Once you learn to think clearly and to speak and write well, you'll be invited into every forest house."

Wintergreen immediately ran off to enroll in a college.

"No ladylike piglet," said Priscilla, straightening her skirt, "would ever invite a wolf into her house. You lied!"

"I know that lies often cover up a mischief or cause one," said Aunt Dagmar, "but my lies may actually do him a lot of good."

"They're still lies," said Priscilla, terribly upset.

"When you don't have a policeman nearby to keep the wolf from the door," said Aunt Dagmar, "you have to make do with whatever you have."

"What do you mean?" asked Priscilla.

"I mean," said Aunt Dagmar, "you tell lies."

So, whenever someone puts something to a use for which it wasn't intended, think of Aunt Dagmar suggesting that "you tell lies," and you will remember the word

UTILIZE

V

In the morning, when the sun rose, sending waves of heat across the plains of Africa, the tickbirds used to gather at all the watering holes to wet their feet in the cool waters and feel the gentle squish of mud between their claws. Insects thick as smoke hovered above the water and made a tasty bird meal. The tickbirds never felt the smallest pang of hunger in their place of paradise.

Timothy Tickbird, the leader of the flock, had spent all his life around the grasslands and muddy water holes, playing among the water buffaloes and the hippos, the rhinos and the elephants, the insects and the croaking frogs. Now old, Timothy and his friends suffered from arthritis. All their bones had turned stiff and brittle; their wings ached and their legs hurt. Their dark brown feathers were graying and their bright red bills were turning pink. Each evening, Timothy and his elderly friends found it harder and harder to take flight and find food, then return to the jungle thicket where they lived in the hole of a baobab tree.

"We must find another way to live," thought Timothy. "The water hole teems with insects, but the wetness makes our arthritis all the worse."

So he decided to ask Joey the water buffalo if they could ride on his back and eat the insects that collected in his hair. But Joey said, "Carry you around! What do you think I am, an elephant?" Wally the hippo also said no, explaining, "I would if I could, but I spend a good deal of time underwater." Timothy flew off to talk to Carol the elephant, who also refused, saying, "I carry great loads for explorers and hunters. I don't carry birds on my back!"

Timothy shrugged and left. He didn't want to disturb Violet the rhino, rolling around in the mud, because everyone asked her for favors. But as he had no other choice, he interrupted her bath.

"Vi," he explained, calling her by her pet name, "if you'll let me and my friends ride on your back, we'll eat the ticks and the worms, the insects and bugs that get inside your ears and under the folds of your skin. And we'll do you an even greater favor than just keeping your skin healthy and clean!"

"What's that?" asked Vi.

"We know you like to sleep most of the day and that even when you're wide awake, you can hardly see your enemies approach. So if you'll let us ride on your back, we'll screech and warn you whenever any danger's near."

"It's a deal!" said Vi.

But no sooner had Timothy made all the arrangements than a few of the tickbirds began to complain that if they rode on Vi and ate from her back, they'd never again feel the splash of water on their legs or the squiggle of mud underfoot.

"Don't worry," said Timothy, "we can hear Vi's hoofs squish through the mud and watch the water splash over her legs. We'll feel all our pleasures secondhand through Vi if we let Vi carry us."

So, whenever someone imaginatively shares in the experience of another, think of Timothy urging the tickbirds to "let Vi carry us," and you will remember the word

VICARIOUS

**W**Dora, Flora, and Nora prided themselves on being copycats. If one of them used eye makeup, or wore purple sneakers without socks, or braided her hair in cornrows, the others did also.

Mrs. Prescott, their homeroom teacher, often teased Dora, Flora, and Nora about being just like one another, but she never worried much about it until the girls began to speak and think the same way. They all repeated the word "like" in every sentence, and the word "cool" every third minute. Good things they called "totally excellent" or "awesome" or "rad"; bad things, "gross" or "icky" or "yucky." If one of the girls praised the rock singer I. D. Klein, the others did too. Since Flora hated geometry, Nora and Dora followed suit.

Finally, Mrs. Prescott decided to have a talk with them.

"Dora, Flora, and Nora," she said rather sternly, "you may think it's cute, or darling, or sweet, or totally excellent to act like copycats, but in fact such behavior makes you appear childish. You behave like sheep following one another off a cliff. The whole point of going to school is to train your minds so that you can think for yourselves and develop your own personalities. Two months from now is the prom. I want you to decide without asking each other's opinion what you are going to wear. The night of the dance, I want to see each of you wearing a different dress. I want to see three dresses, not one. Now's the time to start expressing your own individual tastes."

On the way home from school, Dora, Flora, and Nora agreed not to discuss with one another what they'd be wearing to the dance.

"Let's each pick our own dress," said Nora, "and not tell. That way, no one will know, until the night of the dance, what the others are wearing. What a wonderful surprise it will be."

Dora and Flora promised; then the three of them ran off to pick out their dresses.

On prom night, Mrs. Prescott stood at the door wondering how Dora, Flora, and Nora would dress. The first to arrive was Nora, all decked out in a bright red taffeta dress with billowy sleeves. A few minutes later, Dora arrived in exactly the same bright red taffeta dress with billowy sleeves. Shortly thereafter, Flora arrived, wearing the same bright red taffeta dress with billowy sleeves.

"I thought," said Mrs. Prescott, disappointed, "that each of you was going to choose her own dress, and not once again act like sheep."

"Honest," replied Flora, "we never once talked to each other about our dresses."

"Not once!" repeated Dora.

"It's just an accident," added Nora.

Mrs. Prescott found it all very surprising.

"It's extraordinary," she said, "that you would all choose the same dress to wear to the dance. It's simply amazing. One dress!"

So, whenever something is surprising, extraordinary, or amazing, think of Mrs. Prescott saying, "One dress!" and you will remember the word

WONDROUS

X

After having lived for many years in New Jersey, Mr. and Mrs. Forest retired to Arizona, where they bought a ranch house in the desert. They loved the views of the cacti and mountains, and the vast blue skies. But they didn't like the sand outside their door. They wanted a garden; and having had one in New Jersey filled with bluebells and goldenrod, grass and moist ferns, trees of oak and maple and dogwood and sassafras, they decided to cultivate the same plants in Arizona.

In the spring, they dug holes, turned over the soil, added fertilizer, and soaked the ground. From catalogues they ordered trees, shrubs, ferns, and grass. They could already imagine ripe apples hanging on the branch and luscious flowers drooping on the vine. They could

almost see the laurel grow, and smell the honeysuckle, and feel the grass against their bare feet. They dreamed of an easy life in a green shade.

But once the plants were firmly in the ground, their leaves began to turn from green to brown, as every day the sun grew hotter. Mr. and Mrs. Forest, who were no quitters, fought to save the plants. They struggled with the honeysuckle and the laurel. They built a sprinkler system and watered all the day long. But still the plants browned and wilted. The Forests put up an arbor and then fences to

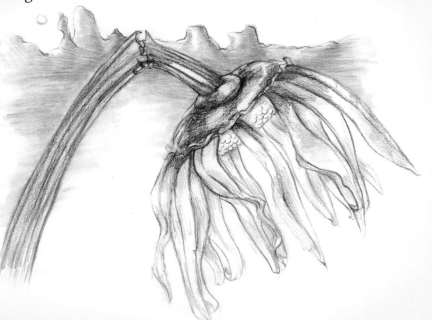

83

screen the sun. Nothing helped. Time and again the trees and plants all died.

By the start of the summer, Mrs. Forest turned to her husband and said, "We have to stop fighting with the plants. We'll never make our garden green."

"But surely," answered Mr. Forest, "there is something we can grow. Other people have gardens in the desert. Let's find out what they have planted."

So they asked Miss Thorne, the local florist.

"In the desert," said Miss Thorne, "there's just one rule for growing things: use plants that can stand the dryness and the heat, plants that don't need much water."

The Forests, acting on this advice, bought a catalogue of desert plants and ordered cacti that looked like organ pipes and coachwhip with lovely scarlet flowers. They sent for prickly pears with yellow blooms and for beardtongue with blue-black blossoms. They also asked for Joshua trees and Indian paintbrush and beaver tail cacti.

In no time at all, the plants arrived and the Forests quickly married them to earth. What a lovely sight the Forests now saw before them, a garden not shaded all in green, but colored in the pastels of the desert.

"How beautiful it is," said Mrs. Forest, "and so much easier to care for."

"Do you remember," remarked Mr. Forest, "how we fought with all those other plants?"

"I certainly do," said Mrs. Forest, "but from now on there'll be no more fighting, because these desert plants are zero fights."

So, whenever plants grow in very dry places, think of Mrs. Forest saying, "These desert plants are zero fights," and you will remember the word

XEROPHYTE

Y

At the top of a tower in a deep forest lived a sorcerer of unusual skill. Dressed in a pointed hat and a purple robe decorated with stars and crescent moons, and cradling in his lap a yellow cat, the sorcerer sat on an ivory chair cushioned with pillows spun from threads of gold. Like all sorcerers, he knew how to make the moon stand still, how to influence the winds, how to turn sand into gold, and how to charm money from a miser. But in addition to these wonderful powers, he had one greater: he could tell which course of action would turn out right in the future.

Strangely, the sorcerer never used a crystal ball or magic wand. His knowledge came not from ghosts or dreams or charms or playing cards, but from the kitchen pantry—from the carrots and the eggs, the peppers and the cheese, the turnips and the lettuce leaves. Gathering up an armful of fruits and vegetables and other foods, he would toss them above his head, and, depending on whether they floated or thudded to the ground, he could tell which future course to take.

Hearing of the sorcerer's skill, a group of knights in silver armor came one day to ask for his advice.

"Will we find the fire-breathing dragon and his chest of gold," they asked, "by following the paths that wander through the marshes or by turning up the mountain?"

The sorcerer threw several items of food in the air.

"All of them, the pepper, celery, and cheese," he said, "have stayed aloft, all except the turnip, which has fallen to the ground. So my advice to you is turn up the mountain."

The knights left at once in search of the fire-breathing dragon and his treasure. Many months later, the knights returned, carrying with them the dragon's chest of gold, which they placed at the foot of his chair. "We have another question," said the knights. "Should we leave the treasure here with you and the cat, or should we take it with us on our journey to the sea? Which place will be the safer?"

Going to the pantry, the sorcerer took from the shelf a head of lettuce, some tomatoes and carrots, and a handful of artichokes and avocados. Throwing them in the air, he stepped back to watch which would float and which would fall.

"The lettuce," said the sorcerer, "has fallen to the ground. So let us, the cat and me, keep the treasure for you."

Two years later, when the knights returned, they found their treasure safe and sound.

"Sorcerer," they said, "you are a wise and honest man. We would like you to join us on our next adventure. We want you to be one of us, a companion and a partner."

The sorcerer, unsure of whether to join the party, went to the kitchen pantry, took several potatoes, an egg, carrots, and yams, and tossed them in the air. Everything floated, including the egg. But the eggshell broke, causing the yolk to fall to the floor.

"What does it mean?" asked the knights. "Will you go with us or not?"

"I will join you and be your companion and partner," said the sorcerer. "The message is clear: the yolk fell low."

So, whenever someone is a companion or mate, think of the sorcerer joining the knights because the yolk fell low, and you will remember the word

YOKEFELLOW

Z

The first time Mr. Al Posner of Brooklyn Heights, New York, tried his hand at business, he built a cement canoe. But his investment, like his canoe, sank and disappeared. The next time, he put his money in lead balloons. But his balloons never got off the ground. In his third attempt at business, he designed a sail-driven car. But his car stalled on windless days.

His newest idea was to start a clothing store for pets and to offer, besides blankets and sweaters, pet garments for the knee. Yes, the knee: for example, knee guards for horses, knee shields for goats, knee socks for dogs, knee warmers for cats, knee woolies for hamsters, and knee quilts for fleas. As a boy, Al had owned a coat and gloves and scarf, but never long pants. His family gave him only knickers; and because the knickers

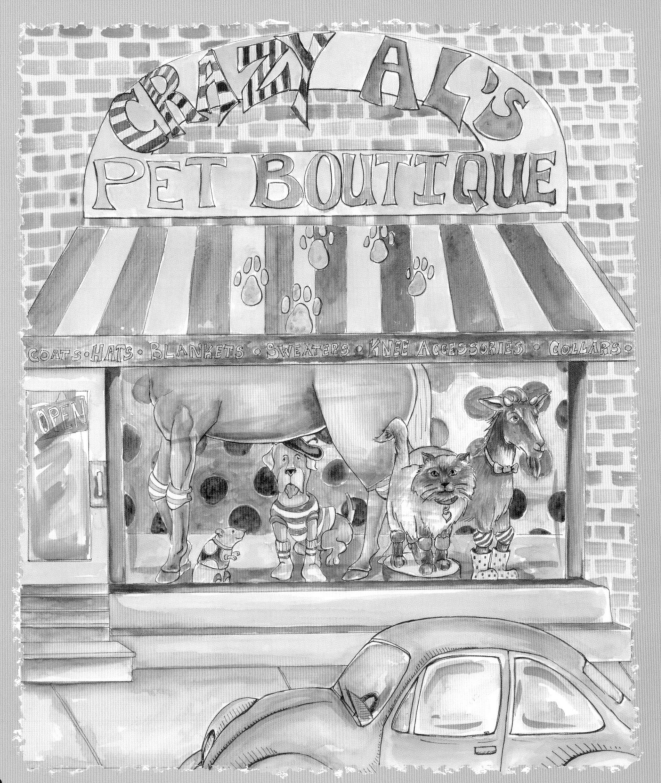

were always secondhand, they never were a proper fit: they never covered up his knees. Remembering how his knees grew red and chapped on wintry days, he told himself that animals must surely know the problem, too.

Not surprisingly, children came from far and wide to see his loony store. But though they loved the different animal clothes that he displayed for sale and the funny knee protectors he designed, what they loved most were the silly little poems that Al composed for them. Whenever children entered Al's shop, he gave them a piece of candy, and on the spot made up a rhyme, something like

> From London sites
> To Brooklyn Heights
> When you see me
> I'll pinch your knee.

Then he'd pretend to pinch the children's knees as they laughed and clapped their hands in merriment.

Al was perfectly happy playing with the kids, but once again his business was failing. He rarely sold animal blankets and booties, and never sold any of his knee clothes. When he asked a little girl who often came to see him in his store what he should do, she said, "Children know all about you, but the grownups don't. Why not write a crazy poem to go along with this crazy store of yours? Tell them what you sell and tell them to ask for Al, the knee nut."

"Not a bad idea," said Al.

"But remember: it has to be really wacko," explained his little friend. "People like foolishness when it's all in fun."

Children, of course, often speak with wisdom; and this girl was especially wise. Al wrote a rhyme, and the people came running to his store to buy knee clothes of every color and design. His rhyme, which he put outside his store, simply said

If you're looking for a store
That offers only bedroom doors

Then ask for Mr. Chest-of-Drawers.
But if you want to clothe a flea,
To cover his extremity,
Then ask for Al, or just say "knee."

So, whenever someone is comical or slap-stick or foolish or crazy, think of Al Posner saying, "Ask for Al or just say 'knee,'" and you will remember the word

ZANY